Money Sense

Managing Money

Andrew Einspruch

A+

Smart Apple Media
P.O. Box 3263
Mankato, MN, 56002

First published in 2011 by
MACMILLAN EDUCATION AUSTRALIA PTY LTD
15–19 Claremont St, South Yarra, Australia 3141

Visit our web site at www.macmillan.com.au or go directly to www.macmillanlibrary.com.au

Associated companies and representatives throughout the world.

Library of Congress Cataloging-in-Publication Data has been applied for

Publisher: Carmel Heron
Commissioning Editor: Niki Horin
Managing Editor: Vanessa Lanaway
Editors: Tim Clarke and Kirstie Innes-Will
Proofreader: Georgina Garner
Designer (cover and text): Kerri Wilson
Page layout: Kerri Wilson
Photo research: Elizabeth Sim (management: Debbie Gallagher)
Illustrator: Chris Dent
Production Controller: Vanessa Johnson

Manufactured in China by Macmillan Production (Asia) Ltd.
Kwun Tong, Kowloon, Hong Kong
Supplier Code: CP March 2011

Acknowledgments
The author and the publisher are grateful to the following for permission to reproduce copyright material:

Front cover photograph: Shutterstock/Diamond_Images, (background), /dibrova (coins), /Gelpi, (boy), /Bianda Ahmad Hisham, (background), /LoopAll, (money bag), /MalDix, (data sheets).

Back cover photograph: Shutterstock/Diamond_Images, (background), /dibrova (coins), /Bianda Ahmad Hisham, (background).

Corbis/Blend Images/Pam Ostrow/Stewart Cohen, **19**, /epa/KAMIL KRZACZYNSKI, **17**, /Golden Pixels LLC/Kai Chiang, **10**, /Jordan/
Whisson, **25**; Dreamstime/Han Cheng Tan, **3** (top), **11**, **30** (bottom); Getty/Jamie Grill Photography, **6** (top), /White Packert, **27**, /PNC,
16 /Derek E. Rothchild, **5** (right); iStockphoto.com/Arpad Benedek, **9**, /Ben Blankenburg, **26**, /Clicks, **14**, /Danny Hooks, **22** (top), /
Sean Nel, **22** (bottom), /Jeffrey Smith, **24**, /Suzanne Tucker, **4**; MEA/Liz Sim, **12**, **13** (bottom left, and right), **30** (top); Photolibrary/
James Hardy /Arunas Klupsas, **20**, /PhotoAlto Agency, **18**, /Lite Productions, **7**, /Dietmar Plewka, **15** (top); pixmac/ktsdesign, **29**;
Shutterstock/Joe Belanger, **21** (top), /Diamond_Images, throughout (background), /dibrova, **1**, /EDHAR, **8**, /Bianda Ahmad Hisham,
throughout (background), /Lipsky, **5** (left), **6** (bottom), **13** (top left), **15** (bottom), /MalDix, **throughout** (background), /Robyn
Mackenzie, **32**, /Monkey Business Images, **28**, /zonesix, **3** (bottom), **21** (bottom).

While every care has been taken to trace and acknowledge copyright, the publisher tenders their apologies for any accidental
infringement where copyright has proved untraceable. They would be pleased to come to a suitable arrangement with the rightful
owner in each case.

Please note
At the time of printing, the Internet addresses appearing in this book were correct. Owing to the dynamic nature of the Internet,
however, we cannot guarantee that all these addresses will remain correct.

Contents

Money Sense 4

Managing Money 5

Earning Money 6

Growing Money by Saving 10

Growing Money by Investing 14

Spending Money Wisely 18

Making a Budget 22

Managing Debt 24

Who Wants to Be a Millionaire? 28

Find Out More 30

Glossary 31

Index 32

Glossary Words

When a word is printed in **bold**, you can look up its meaning in the Glossary on page 31.

Money Sense

Money — it makes sense to know about it. People use money and think about it every day. How much money does this cost? Do I have enough money to buy that? Should I save my money for something? All of the answers to these questions relate to understanding how money works.

Money Matters

Like it or not, money matters. It matters whether people have a lot of money or just a little. How much money people have and how they manage their money both affect the life choices they can make. A decision today, such as saving money or spending it, can affect what they can do months and years from now.

Asking yourself "What does having money let me do?" can help you develop good money sense.

Money is ... a form of energy that tends to make us more of who we already are, whether it's greedy or loving.

Dan Millman, athlete and author

Managing Money

Managing money is a crucial life skill. Being able to manage money can help people avoid problems with money throughout their lives.

Start With Simple Rules

Successful money management can be achieved by following a few simple rules of **financial literacy**:

- Spend less than you earn.
- Save or **invest** part of everything you get.
- The sooner you start growing your money, the easier it is to make a lot of it.
- Money itself is neither good nor bad; what is good or bad is what you do with it.

If people understand these rules, they can begin to manage their money well. They do not even have to be good with numbers!

Financial Literacy

Financial literacy means understanding finances and having the ability to make good decisions about managing money. Like reading and writing literacy, financial literacy is an important skill for life.

Saving money is one of the simple rules of good money management.

Earning Money

Before people can manage their money, they have to learn how to get it! Money that people earn is called **income**. As people become adults, their need to earn money increases. There are three main ways people earn money: working in a job, having a business, and making investments.

Allowances

When people are young and not yet old enough to get a job, their main income may be an allowance from their parents. Sometimes this is in return for doing certain chores for the family. Some parents provide their children with an allowance so they can learn how to handle money. There is no correct amount for an allowance — it depends on the family's circumstances.

Receiving an allowance from their parents can help them start developing good money management skills.

Responsibilities Versus Paid Tasks

It is important to realize that you do not need to be paid for everything you do. Some things have to be done because they are your responsibility as part of a family or a community.

Working in a Job

A job is where someone pays another person to do work. Basically, the person is selling his or her time and skills — the person gets money for spending his or her time at that job and for performing certain tasks. While there is some freedom, the person is generally required to do what the boss wants the person to do.

Jobs for Young People

Most young people begin in jobs that do not require much previous experience or training. These are called entry-level jobs. Restaurant jobs and laboring jobs are popular entry-level jobs, because the tasks and skills involved can be learned on the job.

An entry-level job, such as working at a supermarket, is a great way to start earning money.

Having a Business

When you have a business, you are the boss. Your business provides **goods** or **services** to people who pay for them. It costs you a certain amount to provide these goods and services, and you charge other people more than it costs you. The difference is **profit**.

Being the boss has its advantages. The decisions are yours and if you are successful, you can make a lot more money than you could if you worked for someone else. However, there are also disadvantages and **risks**. Running a business is a lot of work. Also, it is your responsibility if your business does not succeed.

If you are the boss, you have more risks, but you can also gain more rewards.

> Annual income twenty pounds, annual expenditure nineteen ... result happiness. Annual income twenty pounds, annual expenditure twenty ... and six [pence], result misery.
>
> Charles Dickens, *David Copperfield*, 1849

Making Investments

Investing is where you make your money available for others to use. In return, they pay you for the use of the money. That payment is either in the form of **interest** or in a share of their profits. The money you invest is called the **investment**.

Earned Income Versus Passive Income

Earned income is money you earn from a job or business. Passive income is money you get from investments. It is called passive income because you are not actively doing anything to earn it.

Passive income has the advantage of "working" even when you are not working. That is, your investments keep earning money whether you are working, playing, or sleeping. So, having passive income as one way of getting money is a good idea.

It is important to make careful decisions about where to invest your money, as this will affect how your money is used and how much interest you can earn.

Growing Money by Saving

Once you get some money, what should you do with it? While it is fine to spend some of your money, it is a really good idea to hold on to some of your money so you can grow it.

Why Should People Save?

There are several good reasons to save. For one, if you save some of your money, then you will always have some if you need it. You can also put those saved dollars to work, so you earn more money each day and grow richer.

Another reason to save is to gather enough money to do something expensive. This might be buying a new bike or musical instrument, or taking a trip that you always wanted to take. By saving, people can make this kind of thing possible.

Saving helps people gather the money to pay for expensive things, such as a vacation.

Savings Accounts

One of the easiest ways to grow money is to put it into a savings account with a **bank** or similar organization. All banks have several kinds of savings accounts. Some of them "tie up" your money for a period of time (months or years), which means that you cannot use your money during that time, while others let you have it any time you want.

Savings accounts all have one thing in common — they pay the saver interest for the right to hold and use his or her money.

Savings Account

Savings Account

Opening a savings account at a bank or similar organization is one way to grow your money.

If you would (want to) be wealthy, think of saving as well as getting.

Benjamin Franklin, former U.S. president

How Much Interest?

The amount of interest a saver receives when saving his or her money varies, depending on the **interest rate**, how long the person leaves the money with the bank, and how much he or she **deposits**. Generally, the more people deposit and the longer they leave it, the more they earn.

Interest rates change over time, depending on what is happening in the world and what the government is trying to do — either speed up business activity or slow it down. Interest rates are lower if the government wants to encourage business activity, and higher if they want to slow it down.

What Does the Bank Do With the Money?

The bank takes the money a saver deposits and lends it to someone else, such as a business or someone borrowing money to buy a house. They charge the borrower interest on the loan and pay the saver part of what they receive. The difference is their profit.

Banks charge different rates of interest for different loans.

Whatever you want, get there more quickly.

TERM DEPOSIT

6.30 % p.a.

For 10 months on balances from $ 10,000 to $500,000. Available for new and renewing accounts upon request. Interest paid at maturity. If term advertised is longer than 12 months, interest will be paid annually and also at maturity.

Talk to a Savings Specialist today.

Determined to be different

How Much Should a Person Save?

There is no right answer to the question "How much should a person save?" However, an easy rule to follow is "Save 10 percent of everything you get." Ten percent is easy to figure out (It is one dollar out of every ten.). It is not so much that you will miss it from your spending, and it adds up quickly over time.

Remember: Money Is Not Everything

While you are learning to save, remember that money is only part of the happiness puzzle. You also need to love, share, be generous, and be kind to have a happy life.

Saving Tip

Set aside 10 percent before you do anything else with the money you get. Otherwise, it is too easy to spend it.

spend
90 percent

save
10 percent

Saving 10 per cent of what you earn is a simple, effective way to save.

Growing Money by Investing

Investing is where others use your money to do something, such as building a business or buying a house. In return, they pay you for the use of the money, either in interest or as a share of profits. Investing is different from saving, because your money is at risk. That is, you might lose your investment.

Risk in Investing

One of the key ideas in investing is risk. Risk is the likelihood that something will go wrong. In the case of an investment, it is the likelihood that a person will lose his or her money.

All investments involve some level of risk, but not all risk is the same. For example, investing money in a well-established business is typically much less risky than investing money in a new business.

Before investing in something, businesses carefully examine the risk involved.

How Does Risk Relate to Reward?

For investors, risk must be tied to reward. The higher the risk, the more the investor wants to be paid for taking on that risk.

Clever investors usually have many different investments, each of which has a different level of risk. Some of the investments will be "safe" or very low risk, and pay a low, but fairly certain, **return**. Other investments will be riskier, but could provide a greater return.

A lottery ticket is a classic high-risk, high-return investment. People are almost certain to lose their money, but if they win, the rewards are huge.

Measuring Return As a Percentage

You measure your return by comparing it to how much you invest. For example, if you invest $100 and get your money back plus $5, you have made 5 percent. However, if you get your $100 back plus another $100, then you have doubled your money, or made a 100 percent return.

How Fast Does the Return Come?

How much return investors get is only part of the picture. Another part is how quickly or slowly they can expect their return. Receiving a 10 percent return over ten years is less attractive than a 10 percent return over two years.

So, the longer investors have to wait, the greater the reward needs to be, or the lower the risk. This is because the investors could be doing something else with their money instead of having it tied up with that particular investment.

Investors will be willing to make long-term investments if they are confident their money will grow over time.

Examples of Investments

The following are some common investments.

Type of Investment	How It Works	What the Investor Gets Back
Stocks (also called **shares**)	An investor buys shares or stocks, which are small units of ownership in a company.	A small portion of that company's success and profits.
Mutual Funds	Lots of people contribute small amounts of money to a pool of money that is invested and managed by a fund manager. The pool of money can be spread across a wide variety of investments.	A percentage of the profits from the fund's investments. The amount the investor gets depends on how much he or she invested.
Bonds	Bonds are promises to pay a specific amount of money on a specific date. They are issued by governments and large companies. Investors buy the bonds for less than their stated amount, and hold them until the bonds are ready to be paid out.	The stated amount of the bond. For example, an investor might pay $80 for a ten-year bond worth $100. He or she expect to profit $20 in ten years.

Stocks are traded at a stock exchange, where traders aim to make money by buying stocks for a low price and selling them for a high price.

Spending Money Wisely

Once you have earned some money, and saved and invested part of it, you might enjoy spending some of it. However, smart people make sure they get the most value for their money, so their money provides them the greatest benefit.

Looking for Bargains

Bargain-hunting is a great way to get good value for money. The price of something that you want can vary greatly, depending on where you buy it. A bit of research online can help you save a lot of money on the price.

Sometimes you can buy a similar product at a cheaper price. "No-brand" or generic products in supermarkets are a perfect example of this. Often the product is exactly the same, but because there is no brand, it is cheaper.

Buying "no-brand" products can be an easy way to get a bargain.

I have enough money to last me the rest of my life, unless I buy something.
Jackie Mason, U.S. comedian

How to Find a Bargain

Bargains are everywhere if you know where to look. Try looking for them at:

- any store that has a sale on. Good sales are often at predictable times (such as just after Christmas), so you can plan for them
- secondhand stores
- online services where people give things away for free
- online **auctions**

Buying Quality

When spending your money, the quality of the item matters, as well as the price. If something is well made and it will give you a lot of use and pleasure, it can easily be worth paying more than you would for a similar product that is badly made.

Well-made, high-quality goods that will last, such as this bike, are usually worth paying more for.

Impulse Buying

We have all thought "Oh, that would be fun to have!" when we saw certain goods in the stores. Sometimes we act on this thought and sometimes we do not.

Impulse buying is where a person makes a decision to buy something without giving it much thought. Impulse purchases, whether large or small, can use up money quickly.

Avoiding Impulse Buying

Here are some hints for avoiding impulse buying.

- Be careful at checkout counters in stores. Everything there, such as the candy and magazines, is designed to encourage you to buy on impulse.
- Make a shopping list and stick to it.
- Every time you make a purchase, ask yourself, "Do I really need this?"
- If you are thinking about buying something, wait a few days and see if you still want it after this time.

The items at checkout counters in stores are almost always goods meant to be impulse purchases, such as chewing gum and chocolate.

Buying Things That Make You Money

One way to be money smart is to spend your money on things that make you money, instead of spending it on things that take your money away. Although you may not be able to do this while you are young, it is an important thing to understand for later.

A rental property is a good example of something that makes money. It costs money to buy a house, but by renting it to someone else, you may be able to make a profit.

A car is an example of something that keeps taking money away from you. Not only do you pay to get the car, but you also keep paying for gasoline and to keep the car running.

A rental property is something that a person can buy to make money, whereas a car is something that will keep costing money.

FOR RENT

Making a Budget

A budget is a plan for your money, showing how much income you expect to get and what your **expenses** might be. Budgets are a good guide for helping you stay on track financially.

What Is in a Budget?

In a budget, you list all of your income sources and how much you expect to receive from each. Then, you list all of your expenses and how much you expect each to cost. You can then think about whether you can change the way you plan to use your money to get a better result.

A budget does not have to be fancy or difficult, and it does not need to be set in stone. Budgets are plans that can be changed as your circumstances change.

While a budget can be done on paper, if it is done in a spreadsheet, you can easily adjust the numbers to see the effect of different income amounts and spending choices.

Making a Simple Budget

1. List all of your income sources.

2. List all of your expenses.

3. Enter how much you expect to get from each of your income sources.

4. Enter how much you expect to pay for each of your expenses.

5. Subtract total expenses from total income to see how much you have left. This is called the net amount.

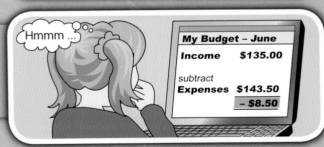

6. Adjust your expense amounts to get a better result.

Managing Debt

For many people, borrowing money (also called going into **debt**) is how they deal with money problems. Debt comes in many forms, including **mortgages**, personal loans, and credit cards.

What Are the Problems with Debt?

Debt always comes at a price. Any time a person borrows money, he or she has to pay interest on it. So, it costs money to borrow money, and the more a person borrows, the more it costs.

Another big problem is borrowing more than a person can actually pay back. Some people get trapped in debt, unable to pay it off. They find themselves stuck in situations where their incomes are too low to pay back everything they have borrowed.

Debt is where people borrow money, such as when a couple takes out a loan.

Credit Cards

Credit cards are an easy way to borrow money. They are convenient to use, but purchases made with them are made with money borrowed from the credit card company, which charges interest.

The interest rates for credit cards are very high compared to other loans. If people do not pay off their credit card quickly, they can end up paying a lot of additional money in interest. Most young people are much better off not getting credit cards.

Debit Cards

Debit cards are like credit cards, except people use their own money instead of borrowing money from a credit card company. Using a debit card instead of a credit card means people are not in debt and do not have to pay interest.

No man's credit is ever as good as his money.
Edgar Watson Howe, U.S. writer

Credit cards can be tempting, but they are also an easy way to get into debt.

Good Debt Versus Bad Debt

Sometimes there are good reasons to go into debt. We can think of debt as either "good" debt or "bad" debt. "Good" debt is a debt that goes toward something that is likely to increase in value over time. Examples of good debt are money borrowed for buying a house, getting an education, or growing a business.

"Bad" debt is pretty much everything else. This includes car loans (cars lose value over time), credit cards, loans for vacations, and almost all other forms of borrowing.

Borrowing money to go to college is one of the few forms of "good" debt, because usually a college education helps people make more money in their working lives after they have graduated.

Tips for Avoiding Debt

Here are some tips that can help you avoid going into debt, especially "bad" debt.

- If you need time to buy something, use **layaway** instead of a credit card.
- Use a prepaid card for your cell phone, instead of paying later. This helps you keep track of how much you are spending.
- Where possible, pay **cash** for things.
- Make sure you save 10 percent of everything you earn.
- Have a goal for your savings and take steps to reach that goal.
- Put your loose change in a jar, then deposit that money into your account once the jar is full.
- Avoid impulse buying. Ask yourself, "Do I really need this?"
- Save for the things you want instead of buying them some other way.
- If you need a card, get a debit card instead of a credit card.

Paying cash is a good way to stay out of debt and be aware of how much you are spending.

Some debts are fun when you are acquiring them, but none are fun when you set about retiring them.

Ogden Nash, U.S. poet

Who Wants to Be a Millionaire?

Part of leading a happy life is leading a happy financial life. Having financial goals and learning to manage your money are both important.

Do You Have a Plan?

How can you go somewhere if you do not know where you want to go? It is the same for your finances. Having a financial plan helps you determine what you want for yourself. Do you want to be a millionaire or just have enough to live comfortably? Either way, you need to think about how you might be able to achieve that goal and then come up with a plan. Whatever you want, the sooner you start, the sooner you will get there.

Making a financial plan helps you determine how you want to manage your money.

Getting to a Million Dollars

Do you want to be a millionaire? Here are some steps you will need to take.

- Learn to earn. You need money to make money, so figure out different ways to earn it.

- Learn about investing. There are a lot of ways to become a millionaire, and learning how to invest is a good place to start.

- Start now. Money invested before you are 30 years old helps you more than money invested after you are 30.

Playing Monopoly™

The popular board game Monopoly™ is actually a good way to learn about finances, debt, and managing money. Successful strategies in Monopoly™ — such as buying properties that make you money, watching how much you spend, and being ready for life's surprise expenses — all help you develop financial literacy.

Making and holding on to enough money to become a millionaire is a challenge, but it may be done with good planning.

Find Out More

Manage your money better by finding out more about saving, investing, and budgeting.

Web Sites

www.fool.com

The Motley Fool web site is a fantastic resource for information about managing money, including saving, investing, and budgeting. Try searching for the article "10 lessons to teach kids about money," or search for "teach kids" to find a number of articles about money basics.

www.italladdsup.org

The It All Adds Up web site about personal finance covers a wide range of topics, from how to save for college to making budgets, saving, and investing.

Places to Visit

If you have never been to a bank — and even if you have — it is worth going in to one to see what information it has. Most banks have brochures that tell you about their products and services, which you can take for free. You can also look online at their web sites for similar information.

If you do not yet have a bank account, consider opening a savings account as a first step.

Glossary

auctions
events where buyers and sellers are brought together and items are sold to the highest bidder

bank
a business that holds and lends money for people

bargain
an item bought more cheaply than expected

cash
coins and banknotes

credit cards
plastic cards that allow the holder to make a purchase and then pay back the card issuer later

debit cards
plastic cards that allow purchases to be made using the holder's money

debt
when someone owes money to someone else

deposits
puts money into an account with a bank or similar organization

expenses
things a person spends money on

financial literacy
having enough information and knowledge to make good decisions about money

goods
things that people can buy and touch

impulse buying
buying things without giving the decision much thought

income
money earned

interest
the amount paid by banks for money deposited with them, or charged for money loaned by them

interest rate
the percentage paid on money that is borrowed or deposited

invest
make money available to others to do something

investment
money that someone gives to others in exchange for interest or a share of profits, so the person can grow it

layaway
an arrangement where the buyer can pay for an item in a series of payments

mortgages
loans taken out to buy houses or properties

profit
the difference in money between what a business charges people for goods and services, and what it costs the business to provide those goods and services

return
the money a person gets back from an investment

risks
likelihood of things going wrong, such as suffering losses

services
things that people do for other people

shares
another term for stocks

stocks
small units of ownership in a company

Index

A

allowances 6, 23

B

banks 11, 12, 30
bargains 18, 19
bonds 17
borrowing money 12, 24, 25, 26
budgets 22–23, 30
businesses 6, 8, 9, 12, 14, 26

C

credit cards 24, 25, 26, 27

D

debit cards 25, 27
debt 24–27, 29

E

earned income 9
earning money 5, 6–9, 10, 12, 13, 18, 27, 29
entry-level jobs 7
expenses 22, 23

F

financial literacy 5, 29
financial plan 28

G

goods 8, 19, 20

I

impulse buying 20, 27
income 6, 9, 22, 23, 24
interest 9, 11, 12, 14, 24, 25
investing 5, 9, 14–17, 29, 30
investments 6, 9, 14, 15, 16, 17

J

jobs 6, 7, 9

L

layaway 27

M

money sense 4
Monopoly 29
mutual funds 17

P

passive income 9
profits 8, 9, 12, 14, 17, 21

R

risk 8, 14, 15, 16
rules for money 5

S

saving 4, 5, 10–13, 14, 18, 27, 30
savings accounts 11, 14, 30
services 8, 19, 30
shares 17
spending money 4, 5, 10, 13, 18–21, 22, 27, 29
stocks 17